WHY DID GOD CREATE US?

RAY WEAVER SR.

WestBow
PRESS®
A DIVISION OF THOMAS NELSON
& ZONDERVAN

Copyright © 2017 Ray Weaver Sr.

All rights reserved. No part of this book may be used or reproduced by any means, graphic, electronic, or mechanical, including photocopying, recording, taping or by any information storage retrieval system without the written permission of the author except in the case of brief quotations embodied in critical articles and reviews.

Scripture taken from the King James Version of the Bible.

Scripture taken from the New King James Version®. Copyright © 1982 by Thomas Nelson. Used by permission. All rights reserved.

Scripture taken from the American Standard Version of the Bible.

Scripture quotations taken from the New American Standard Bible® (NASB), Copyright © 1960, 1962, 1963, 1968, 1971, 1972, 1973, 1975, 1977, 1995 by The Lockman Foundation Used by permission.

Scriptures taken from the Holy Bible, New International Version®, NIV®. Copyright © 1973, 1978, 1984, 2011 by Biblica, Inc.™ Used by permission of Zondervan. All rights reserved worldwide. www.zondervan.com The "NIV" and "New International Version" are trademarks registered in the United States Patent and Trademark Office by Biblica, Inc.

WestBow Press books may be ordered through booksellers or by contacting:

WestBow Press
A Division of Thomas Nelson & Zondervan
1663 Liberty Drive
Bloomington, IN 47403
www.westbowpress.com
1 (866) 928-1240

Because of the dynamic nature of the Internet, any web addresses or links contained in this book may have changed since publication and may no longer be valid. The views expressed in this work are solely those of the author and do not necessarily reflect the views of the publisher, and the publisher hereby disclaims any responsibility for them.

Any people depicted in stock imagery provided by Thinkstock are models, and such images are being used for illustrative purposes only. Certain stock imagery © Thinkstock.

ISBN: 978-1-9736-0638-3 (sc)
ISBN: 978-1-9736-0640-6 (hc)
ISBN: 978-1-9736-0639-0 (e)

Library of Congress Control Number: 2017916606

Print information available on the last page.

WestBow Press rev. date: 10/30/2017

Ray Weaver Sr. Previous Books

"A Search for The Truth"
Published by WestBow Press a division of Thomas Nelson and Zondervan, Released in July 30, 2014

"The Alpha to the Omega"
Self-published February 16, 2011 to alphabetically emphasizing short pages on each letter in English alphabet of humans and the attributes of God's perfection.

"MMMA Test Strategy/Guidelines for Aerospace Vehicles"
Published by Martin Marietta Michoud Aerospace, released in April 30, 1986

Covers all technical aspects of design, fabrication and testing for aerospace components through vehicles technically, relevant to that time period. Guidelines for Space Station Proposal preparation.

CONTENTS

Preface ix

Chapter 1: "Why" 1
Chapter 2: What We Know 13
Chapter 3: What Is Really Correct? 23
Chapter 4: Accident Or On Purpose 31
Chapter 5: Why Was All This Done 41
Chapter 6: What Are We To Do 47
Chapter 7: Gods Holy Bible 53
Chapter 8: Conclusion 85

Basic Biblical Truths 91
Contributors and Thanks to All 95
Ray Weaver Sr.'s Background 97

PREFACE

This book was written as a continuation of "A Search for Truth" by Ray Weaver Sr.

Hopefully it will answer or at least stimulate thinking toward why we are here in the first place. To provide guidance in how we think and act, plus what to look forward to depending on choices we make in our short time here on earth.

When we think in terms of centuries, millenniums, etc. our time here is very short, how much impact do we really make or mean in the larger scheme of things. Are we really important at all? Our time and opportunities to make an impact may be very short or long depending on our life time and what we do with it, food for thought, future planning and action.

Mainly a long term eternal plan and not just for the

present here and now. Not like our worldly philosophies and education systems have taught for years and teach today in school and life.

I believe God is telling us and showing us the way, the truth and the life we are to live and is helping guide us by the Holy Spirit. It does not mean the path will be easy, but it will be per His will and way, which is all that is important.

Trust in the Lord with all your heart (mind and soul) and lean not on your own understanding, in all your ways submit to Him and He will make your pathway straight. (Proverbs 3:5-6) KJV

Note: All direct biblical references will be annotated by Bible, Book, Chapter and Verses referenced, (All will be from KJV, NKJV, ASV, NASV, and NIV). In many cases I'll just reference book, chapter and verse or verses, at the end of reading or as a reference. After reading "A Search for Truth" hopefully you will look it up as necessary in your Bible of choice. In many cases I have not referenced exact verses or summarized in my own words the referenced biblical text along with it. These I will not give Bible used but they will always be from one of the above referenced: KJV, NKJV. ASV. NASV, NIV. I may use an abbreviation or part of a verse and may add some portion of a song as a reference that most of us know already.

CHAPTER 1

"WHY"

"Why" is the great question that all Philosophers ask.
Not how did it happen, but why did it all happen. Why is probably more important than how. The reasoning or wisdom behind the Why everything exists and the reason or purpose to it all is more important than the how it occurred. How is important, do not get me wrong, but the Why actually helps explain the how. How to do something is always important and the how to accomplish anything is important but the larger more significant question of WHY do it, or should it be done at all or is it ethical to do it. Those are bigger more significant questions, yes?

In this great big world and larger universe what makes everything relevant? The universe is immense, with a great number of galaxies, stars (suns), solar systems, etc. and our world has how many different species, along with how many people of all different types, colors, cultures, religions, intellectual levels, histories, genealogies, etc.? What and Why are each important and were each brought into existence, and yes how did it occur?

Again, what makes you or me significant or matter at

all? What are we here for? Why are we here at all? Why do we ask these type questions?

What is the purpose of life, learning, achieving, and survival? What drives us and makes us want to survive, achieve, get ahead, etc.? A lot of people apparently do not even question the answer, or at best **blow it off as what difference does it make**, or just try to be as happy as you can and get as much out of life as you are able to. Some grow up just trying to survive, because the world they grow up in is so harsh. Of course some give up, do not care, or just try to survive it all, while some totally give up. They do not even try to have a chance at any kind of a future or life. How many lives are in constant depression or commit suicide or at least try to? It can occur for many reasons in life, but that is not part of a natural plan as it is giving up, which is not a natural thought out solution. It is not a solution but running away. It is what drives some to drink or use drugs, etc., just to escape.

I believe we were born (created if you will) with an innate desire to survive, along with a desire to figure life out. I'll even go so far as to say that all life forms have a basic desire to survive. Just look at a new baby bird or puppy, they are trying to investigate and figure it all out and want their basic needs satisfied. Even small fish try to stay away from larger fish that want to eat them. It is a natural built in instinct to all living life forms to survive.

This also means our basic instinct is to first survive and then to seek out answers that make sense and are truthful,

We naturally are looking to satisfy this void or eternal question **why me** & then **why this world** as we know it? **What is this life all about?** Natural questions that all people want answered.

Where should we begin this quest?

The following includes a search for that truth with some philosophical answers, along with what I believe are some common sense answers along with various information from numerous sources.

First, if we just accidentally arrived here by pure chance, exist and die by pure chance, it all seems rather futile, except to just do the best we can with what we have been given. That would put us a little better off than an intelligent rock, because we would be able to do some things to improve our situation, but obviously would not control very much of the more important activities of life i.e.:

A. Heritage: physical, mental, chemical, capabilities, tendencies and weaknesses;
B. Family or Country we were born into;
C. Financial situation we were born into;
D. Century or time we were born into;
E. Language, culture, etc.
F. What tomorrow will bring or how we will end up physically, mentally, emotionally, or dare I say spiritually, and on and on with more questions that we do not control or have any power over at all.
G. Climate, weather, earthquakes, etc., and why some are at the wrong place at the wrong time? Coincident, luck or just bad luck, you call it? From one great source it says "It rains on the just and the unjust alike" or another way of saying it is (If you're at a location and bad weather/war/etc. occurs then your caught in it, does not matter who you are)

Second, if we can get past one (that we were not brought into life purely accidentally or by chance) where are we going, short term and long term or even eternally? If you agree with The Holy Bible you already accept, that there will be an afterlife/eternal life. The question is where will it be and why?

This goes back to the basic question does it all go back to our Heavenly Father, Son and Holy Spirit? The Holy Bible refers to all life forms and the entire universe. Who named all the animals by God's directions? ADAM! Who named all the stars? GOD! Look at first part of Genesis.

<u>What is the purpose for It all?</u>

I do not presume to know all the answers to every question and I believe anyone who says they do is not thinking very logically. In fact as I get older and learn more about a lot of different subjects, I find there is so much more to learn and that there are more subjects out there to learn about. Almost everything we have ever studied: Math, Science, Space, Philosophy, Politics, Government, Religion, Geology, Electronics, Mechanics, Physical/Medical Health, and History, you name it. If we keep studying it and as time on this earth passes we learn there is more that we don't know than what we do. Yes, we are smarter than our ancestors were in general, but not necessarily in all cases as we look back on all cases. It has been said "those who do not study or know history are bound to repeat some of the same mistakes all over again".

One of my bosses that had just promoted me into management gave me some great advice. "He told me to take all the facts available into consideration, make a DECISION and then drive on. If you make a mistake, learn from it and do not make the same mistake again, but make the best decision you can at the time and move on". That helped me in the following 38 years of aerospace management and life.

<u>Anyway, I believe there is a purpose for it all and for us, individually and collectively.</u> Life is not futile and it has a purpose or at least was meant to have a purpose! Mankind has definitely messed it up big time over the years, decades, centuries, etc. Usually we have done this for noble reasons or we thought they were noble reasons at the time, but they all boil down to survival, greed, power, and selfishness, which I will call "ME'ism or "US'ism". Sometimes it could be to help others pure and simple, but not many in the world today ever fall into this last category. That could include our family, friends, country, etc. that we want to protect, provide for, help out, because we care for them and hopefully to share God's love for us and pass it on.

Why are we not more giving and forgiving goes back to Me-ism.

There are many other isms that spring out of these same basic instincts and sources such as: protectionism, governments (Democracy, Republics, Kingdoms, Tribes, etc.), feudalism, nationalism, socialisms, communism, fascism, totalitarianism, racism, capitalism, etc. of all types.

I will include Religionism, which is my made up word for all the various religions of the world and attempt by man to reach or at least touch or explain a supreme being/beings and the purpose behind everything, including our existence?

I will not include atheism as that is a complete reversal, which makes each individual a god unto themselves. The atheist thinks he is the ruler of his own destiny at best, or at worst takes us back to being that intelligent rock. Both, I'm god or I'm an intelligent rock that just accidentally showed up, are ridiculous. That is why their special holiday is "April Fool's Day" as they have no purpose to be alive or exist other than to take up space and resources and try to survive the best they can. Atheists choose to be intelligent animals that accidentally arrived and will become nothing but dirt, which also was an accident in their minds to start with. It is not a religion, as it is a belief in nothing or at best a belief in self. <u>That is some philosophy of life, yes?</u> They cannot realistically say it is based on science, because even science and mathematics are based on some logical reasoning and fundamental concepts that are linked to searching for answers and sprang out of philosophical thought searching for the answers of why and how. Atheism, is not trying to understand or seek answers to reality, it assumes there is no reasoning or question of WHY do we exist or this universe exist. They believe it just happened accidentally, so they are mere accidents of an accidental nature and world. Don't know about you, but I'm not interested in being an accident or believing what other accidents think or try to impose on others.

    I think you will all agree this world has been and is a mess. The humans of this world have created a real mess of it all. Some have done better than others but we are all part of the problem. Why, back to that me'ism problem and trying to survive or get ahead our way, the best we can.

    What is the solution to it all? So for the time being let's jump over some of the great issues of debate such as the universe, this world/earth, and creation, as we are

WHY DID GOD CREATE US?

finite earthlings on this small planet, in a small solar system in just one of many galaxies in the universe. It is like an ant trying to explain our earth and its meaning, beginning, and the whys and wherefores of their existence.

CHAPTER 2
WHAT WE KNOW

Let's start at the very beginning - What we do know

Let's go back to the basics. We were born as babies and know nothing except our new environment. We have experienced some life in the womb which we will not recall consciously, but may have some influence on our early nurturing and personality per some Psychologist and Physiologist. We are not sure about all this, but let us say it does have some small effect on us. The other dominant traits we will be endowed with will be what we inherit from our mother and father's linage: traits, tendencies toward, intelligence level, physical attributes; color of hair, eyes, skin, possible allergies, physical weight, height, structural tendencies, etc. etc.

We all want to be warm, fed, clothed, cleaned up, or have all our basic needs met. We all are born selfish and self-centered, and my examples here are fairly simple. You have to teach children to share, and not to be possessive, to be considerate of others and not self-centered. Almost all of the traits to get along with other people and society have to be taught, because our natural instinct is me'ism, that is back where we started from, remember? We do not want to share our food, toys, etc. Why did Adam and Eve take the forbidden fruit? They wanted more, when they had everything they needed without it, and were tempted/desired to know more. We are greedy and self-serving by nature.

I believe it was all part of God's plan and he knew it would happen. He even provided a solution to our problem way back then (Reference John 1). We do have free will and I believe were meant to have. All people have had free will, but look what that cost us all. Our decisions will have consequences on ourselves, others and our off springs.

Next we start learning life's lessons from our parents or the situation we were born into. No one has exactly the same situation from birth or environments such as family makeup, homes, siblings, family life styles, and societies are not identical. Not even if we are in the exact same family, let alone in different parts of the world. Needless to say, there are variables in life that we all face, all of which has an effect on our abilities and thinking processes. We have little to no control of the starting point of our earthly existence.

Our world starts out very small around our primary

care people. Hopefully family and in a home or facility provided by them. We eventually are influenced by a larger and larger world outside that facility and it usually gets expanded more and more as we experience more of the world. We must learn to interact with other people in our family, neighborhood, society, etc. We may even learn about some aspects of a particular religion and a style of government.

Most people seem to get totally absorbed in surviving, their family, education, occupations, jobs, sports, politics, etc. Of course much of life must be involved in some of those things.

Maslow's Law explains some of the priorities in life, as we must have basic survival needs answered before we can start reasoning about other things. It is basically a five tier evaluation of mankind's "Hierarchy of Needs", which at the bottom starts with survival and ends up at the top with altruism as a person reaches the top level. They then have time and ability to be more concerned about others, as the individual is satisfied with their own desires and can afford to be altruistic in nature to others. Another way of saying this is that a person who is starving or freezing is not concerned about where the world or universe came from. They just want food and a warm place to survive. A person, on the other hand who has the necessities of life, including some extra time can stop and reason what is this all about and why. Note: Necessities of life vary drastically by different individuals. Some are happy with a lot less than others, but true necessities are the same for everyone: food, clothing, health, and shelter.

Children immediately start picking up differences in people, such as mannerisms, sounds, appearances, and physical capabilities. They immediately develop likes and dislikes plus they all uniquely learn and develop at different rates.

The children's interactions, even the rank in the pecking order (oldest, youngest, or middle child in a family) makes a difference in their development. Are they introverted or extraverted, quiet or loud, physically dominant or weak and how they adapt to varying situations? Another set of traits that will determine how they develop is how they adapt, such as do they learn by doing, observing or both? Are they able to adapt by using their skills (brain over brawn or vise versa)? Are they questioning by nature and do their parents or guardians respond by teaching them or by shutting them down? Are they determined to find the answers and get results without giving up easily? All questions that set patterns of learning, thinking and developing that influence our future skills, reasoning and abilities. Sometimes I wished I had paid more attention when I was young, but as I grew up physically and mentally I learned it was better to know than not to know. Life is important, all life and aspects of life are important.

Were you nurtured and taught or shut off or did you search on for answers & strive forward anyway or take the easy way out. Probably a little of all the above.

If you have tendencies to be better at mathematics and logic verses languages skills and the arts, you will attack life differently. Of course some people are good at many different skill sets therefore their learning skills will be more adaptable and more diverse.

If you were raised in a very structured controlled environment verses a leis-a-fare environment your reasoning or approach to life will be different. Our minds are capable of overcoming weaknesses and circumstances that may not be ideal, but will have some effect on our thinking from the circumstances we grew up under and how we adapt. What things draw your interests and that you desire to learn about? What ones turn you off or on?

Why did I go through all this to get to the subject of WHY?

Because you're thinking or thought processes have a bearing on how you will perceive the following information. It also gives us a little bit of the same starting point for the discussion that follows. At least I hope it will allow you to perceive where I am coming from and why I believe the way I do. Maybe you will identify with the thought process and relate to it, agree or disagree with it. At least think about it.

Life as we know it varies drastically as previously stipulated, but now let us consider some more questions as to WHY. For example: what is right and wrong, moral or immoral, kind or hateful, love or hate, caring or don't give a hoot about anything or anybody else. Our society has lost the meanings of these words and issues. We may be wrapped up in sports, entertainment, art, science, literature, politics, etc.

The world is great or terrible depending on your outlook and circumstances. God is real or not for many people which leaves them little to look forward to or help them through tough times. Also their age is a bearing on it all (young, teenagers, early 20s-30s, middle age, or old timers and I'll say over 60, when they start seeing more of their friends dying or suffering with tough ailments. Our thoughts and outlooks do change over our life time through experiences or new concerns. The point is that most of us change our outlook and thinking as we learn and mature. A lot of variables and whys to answer or seek to answer from our finite minds and view of the world we exist in. Some learn quicker than others or have better opportunities to learn about life's meaning, purpose, and God.

Some we will never figure out completely period. We will just run out of time and mental capability to understand or absorb it all.

CHAPTER 3
WHAT IS REALLY CORRECT?

"What" do we do to start reasoning through all the WHY's?

We can start by considering all of known human history,

People groups, religions, governments, etc.? Another route would be to start by studying everything we know about our physical world or universe. Philosophers, Scientist, and Scholars over history have tried to accomplish it. In any case it would take a life time just too barely get started or scratch the surface. Many brilliant people have tried to do some of that and come up with their own ideas, theories, hypothesis, etc., but almost all have their ideas updated, changed or proven wrong over time. It is like going back to that "ant" trying to understand our world in totality. So where do we start? Most animals or living creatures just try to survive.

One night my seven year old son was saying his prayer at bed time and asked me "Who created GOD"? My simple answer was he has always existed from minus infinity to plus infinity, therefore will always exist and has always existed. He did not follow up with how did

I know that, but could have. I believe he trusted my answer and temporarily satisfied his question. Reference Revelation 21:6 "He is the Alpha and Omega", which means in Greek the Beginning and the End. (All Bible versions)

Mankind has always debated about a god or gods throughout human history and in our modern age many don't think about it, therefore back to being an intelligent rock. Kind of a sad joke. What does the modern age have to do with any of it? What we know today will be different tomorrow. So, what in this so called modern age have to do with any of it, as it will all continually be changing? What is real and does not change? If you have an electronic or engineering background as I do, there have been constant changes over many years and it seems to be getting faster not slower. How far can it go? When I was working on the Space Shuttle External Tank Program we had Robots and that was way back in the 1970s. Today we would not even classify them as robots. In the Apollo Moon Program we also had Fiber Optics, which most people even today do not know about. These were used in the Apollo Moon first stage (S-1C) back in the 1960s. Fiber Optics were some of the early ways to communicate between continents under the ocean before that, but most people didn't know that. Many people think they are a lot smarter, but are they really when it comes to the total perception of what life is all about, let alone keeping up with rapid changes in science?

Science is updated, changed as new discoveries occur. The physical world and nature changes over time by earthquakes, tsunamis, plate tectonics, weather patterns, volcanoes, etc. Mankind has caused some changes by moving plants and animals from one part of the world to another and by modern application of chemicals, etc.

We have changed the atmosphere to some degree by cutting down too many trees which created oxygen and we have obviously introduced extra chemicals into the atmosphere. All have an effect on this world as we know it. Some cause improvements and some create potential disasters. No one can really know the total effect of all this as the world has been changing on its own for many millenniums. I remember when we were in Fairbanks, Alaska and I was in USAF in the dead of winter it might be in the -50 to -60 degrees below zero in town or on Ladd AF Base. Just a little outside of town it would be -70 or more below zero. If you were outside of town and looked back at it you could see the haze over the city from the heat generated by mankind trying to stay warm. Did not matter what the heat source was, we humans needed to stay warm and the larger the population anywhere will create more atmospheric activity heat, etc. causing some atmospheric changes to some degree. That heat could be carbon based, wood burning, or electricity, whatever. That heat will affect the atmosphere in the immediate area. Even more paved areas thus less grass and greenery will cause it to be hotter or colder depending on light and darkness and weather conditions. Even atomic power generates heat, potential nuclear radiation and presents water problems, plus presents a potential huge problem (Chernobyl). This all will add to less oxygen and allow other chemicals and hazards to have greater effect on life. Yes, mankind has an effect on the weather/climate, but so do other things as stated above.

Will climate change over time, yes? How much and from what and how fast is debatable. The world has obviously gone through many cycles: ice ages, major volcano irruptions into the atmosphere, etc. If you think plate tectonics is over, look at Sweden. The docks the Vikings used hundreds of years ago are now 200 feet above the water as Sweden is gradually getting higher in the air, because of shifting plates (one going under the other). That is referred to as Plate tectonics, which is continents and ocean floors, etc. shifting over time.

So, yes humans do effect our world more and more as there becomes more of us and new inventions and advancements could increase the cycle rates, but how much and how fast is a big question. Does it happen in days, years, or centuries? Your guess is as good as anyone else's, as we can only really look at a very short spectrum of earth's cycles. What is a few hundred years or even 6,000 years compared to millions of years? Does every country cooperate of course not? So how can anyone country or a few countries have much affect

Each species also has a purpose: some provide food and others provide clothing. Yet others help clean up the place such as buzzards, mice and yet others help cultivate plants, such as bees.

So let us look at another idea that might make more sense to it all.

CHAPTER 4

ACCIDENT OR ON PURPOSE

Could it all just happen accidentally? I don't think so!

<ins>Let's look at the question of God</ins>

How were the heavens and earth started and for what purpose? This is a question that has been debated and considered since mankind has existed. So let us ask ourselves some logical questions with hopefully some logical answers. Note: This was covered somewhat completely in the previous book.

> A. Can a manmade god, statue, animal, the sun or moon and stars, or a black rock in Mecca, do anything for us? Don't think so! Imperfect mankind cannot truly mentally or scientifically prove any of it! For sure none of those things do anything for us. Reference The Christian Holy Bible, in Romans 1: 20-23 pretty well covers it. Mankind became so wise in their own mind they started worshipping stars, moon, animals, volcanos, statues, rocks, etc. Pretty stupid don't you think, when God in all His glory is self-evident to anyone that is not blind to reality. The

results are also self-evident Romans 1:18, 19, plus some of the results (read the rest of Romans 1).

B. I believe God is self-evident and human beings do their own thing regardless, because they want to control their own destiny, and not be subservient to a Supreme Being. There is that Me-ism again. Israel got into trouble over and over when they walked away from our heavenly Father (God), look at the Old Testament. Other people groups also were in constant upheaval over and over when man tried to control everything or worshipped non-gods.

C. If we don't want to be just intelligent rocks we must first believe there is something greater than we are. We can't even solve our own problems in this world without killing each other. We really have very little control of our own lives and circumstances we grew up in or live in without God. His internal peace He will give us if we have accepted His Grace and Salvation plan, which is an eternal plan for us now and forever. The Holy Bible is full of examples of this message and especially in the New Testament.

D. Many very smart people have agreed something or someone created/started it all and controls it according to His desires. That identity is far superior to our limited finite minds and abilities. Satan thought he was greater than God and he and a third of the angels were thrown out of heaven for challenging God and His plans. (See G below)
E. Two or more gods would be a problem. It would cause chaos, like we have. Which one to follow, honor and obey, if any at all?
F. A Bad God would even make less sense, as he would not really care about us down here on this little planet, except as play toys or entertainment. Satan is the great deceiver and wants to lead us away from God the Father, or at best make us less effective witnesses!
G. A Good, Loving God and Creator would want the best for us and want us to return His love. He would also have a plan for us in the short and long run, don't you think? Do we have free will? I believe we do and we are supposed to have. We should be seeking Him and wanting to serve Him. He will reward those who diligently do that (Ref. Hebrews 11:6) (KJV)!

We must first put our hopes and trust in Him (Ref. Hebrews 11:1) KJV! Note: Even the angels had free will and one third went astray. When God threw out Satan Rev.12:4 (KJV) "Satan's tail swept 1/3 of stars from the sky and flung them down to the earth" (1/3 of angels). This is the general theological explanation of this verse. Of course Satan was an angel of the highest order before being thrown out of heaven. Some Theologians believe he was Jesus brother. I don't agree but will leave that as a subject to be determined. All I know is Jesus was the Messiah, was God's Son and is part of the Trinity and Satan sure isn't!

H. If we chose a loving God who has a plan for us both for now and forever, then we have hope and an eternal life to look forward to. How great is that? It does not mean all will be rosy down here as mankind has rejected Him and His ways. Therefore, we all will suffer some of the consequences of this evil world.

I. Does He want us to get along with His creation and other people? Obviously, yes! Why would He put us here otherwise? We are to Husband this world and its creatures. Ref. Gen.1:28 (KJV) in the beginning and Gen. 9:1 (KJV) in Noah's time after the flood. The same statements and same Hebrew words are used. We are to replenish the earth not destroy it. Of course we are to use the resources He provided us, but not wipe it out or destroy it. He has set up a lot more for us than we think about. Also, His perfect sacrificial lamb (Jesus) would not have opened His heart to us sinful people, if He did not plan for our way back to Him as part of His Family.

J. Think about it and talk to other people and especially other Christians about it. Not about opinions but His Word "The Holy Bible". The Holy Bible is God's Word. It explains a lot of it, but we must first believe God exists and seek to know Him and what He wants! Reference Hebrews 11:6, actually the whole chapter.

K. It provides the only long term answers for the here and now, but for the eternal plan. Note: All other approaches lead to dead ends and eventual loss of identity to everything except suffering and pain in Hell! Or if your that intelligent rock, that's all folks. According to scripture, God will judge us all one day at his Great White Throne!

Hopefully covered by His son's sacrificial loving, grace gift, if we accept Him and then serve Him by producing fruit (Others Accepting Him).

L. There are many religions or lack of religion, philosophies, and ideas out there in this world, but all, leave gaping holes in their thoughts/ideas. They also do not provide long term solutions that make any sense. Seek the truth AND THE TRUTH WILL SET YOU FREE! (John 8:31,32) KJV. Some have solutions for men only and women don't count. Pretty absurd don't you think? In my case all the women in my life were extremely smart, either with logical thought, Biblical Godly knowledge and instincts, and most were straight ' 'A' students and have common sense. I have worked for and had women work for me in the Space industry that were very intelligent. None were definitely not inferior to men. Some men may be bigger and physically stronger generally and biblically are to lead their families. But that was their assignment (To be men of God and lead), but women/wives are to be their equal partners in leading their families and helping others.

Note: None of what I am referring to has to do with race, color of skin, or sex of an individual. All I have known, worked with, and have worked for personally. They were all good leaders or workers, intelligent, and equally endowed. Likewise, I have worked in church with many of these same type people that were believers and I consider to be my brothers and sisters in Christ. No discrimination, period. The God I worship and believe in does not discriminate except against sin and not accepting Him, Amen.

M. We are to replenish the earth not destroy it. Of course we are to use the resources He provided us, but not wipe it out or destroy it.
N. Our families are to be taken care of.
O. We are to serve God all the days of our lives with His Holy Spirit's guidance.
P. Going to church and sitting there and listening isn't serving or using our God given talents to serve. If we are to pick up our own cross and follow Jesus, means go to work representing and sharing His love.

CHAPTER 5

WHY WAS ALL THIS DONE

<u>My thoughts:</u>

The Holy Bible does not directly tell us, so the following are some possible explanations.

I believe The Trinity decided to do it (see the first part of Genesis) to expand His kingdom and share His love, because He is love and the Light for all of created existence.

Maybe His kingdom was partly lost when Satan and 1/3 of the angels left His kingdom due to their own arrogance, which left a hole in His kingdom. Maybe He missed them because He cares for all and wants all to be part of His kingdom, but being a Holy God He cannot accept sin and rebellion. Consider the wedding feast of the Lamb, where many were invited but some did not come so He invited others to join in the feast. This usually is used to describe allowing Gentiles and other people into His family?

The Trinity knew what Adam and Eve would do and thus mankind would do. Why because God is an all knowing God. The plan to overcome the problem was already set in place for those who would gladly come join and return His love and plan. Of course we individually must by free will choose Him and His way.

I believe He is "The Alpha and Omega" and always has been and will be.

I'm just one of those ants trying to figure it all out and trusting in His Holy Word and Holy directions from the Holy Spirit leading me.

We must first believe He exists either by intuitive thought and observation, led by His Holy Spirit and by other people sharing Him with us "How are they to know unless someone goes and tells them". Then repent and accept Him as our Lord and Savior. After that we must follow His Word which requires us to serve Him by sharing His love with others. The book of James emphasizes works, but we must remember it was written to believers. Works should follow Salvation and acceptance of our Lord and His Grace. Works without His Spirits leading does not count, Reference Christ saying too many who did a lot of works "I don't know you." In Revelation.

The fields are full and plentiful with grain, but someone needs to go and help harvest it for His Glory. We are His servants to do the work in this physical universe, even if it means dying for others and Him.

His Spirit will lead us and show us the way if we are paying attention. Christ already showed us "The Way, The Truth and The Life", we just need to trust and obey as there is no other way but to trust and obey and be happy in Jesus.

We don't do this in our own strength as we are weak, but in His power guided by The Holy Spirit. Christ told us all things are possible to those who love the Lord and serve according to His purpose.

Why did He do all this is a good question, along with why even try to deal with foolish mankind? I believe the above gives some rational thought that makes sense along with His great love, goodness, ability and desire to share what He has for all of us.

I would be skeptical of anyone or manmade religion that contradicts The Holy Bible or tries to argue one verse against another to prove a point that they happen to disagree with. You must look and consider information from The Bible in its entirety. We are not to add or take away from it or adjust it to suit our own purposes. That is a sin in itself per scripture, which is written in scripture at the end of the book of John.

CHAPTER 6

WHAT ARE WE TO DO

Things to look forward to

First — Eternal life with Him and help this world to be a better place to live in for everyone.

Second — Help others survive here, now and for the future with Him, by accepting His Grace and Love offering.

Third — To serve Him and His plan and purpose. How, you might say? By studying His Word and listening to the Holy Spirit's advice and directions and not lean on our own understanding. That can only occur after we repent and totally accept Him. After which we will receive His Holy Spirit to help us and council us (Ephesians 1:13 and Romans 9:37-39). Then go to work using the unique talents He gave us. (Romans 10:9) (Proverbs 3:5-6) and the book of James.

Why would God care for us in the first place?

a. God is Love. Ref. The total book of John and the rest of scripture.

b. He created us, reference the first part of Genesis with attributes like the Trinity has (Body, Mind and Soul).

c. Live according to His plan, which is to follow His example. He became a servant for us to show us the way and loved us enough to die for us. Look at Christ's life and the words spoken at the Lord Supper

So why is that true?

This world as we know it will pass away just like earthly life will, but God (Trinity) is eternal and wants all His created children to love Him and be with Him. Do you know any other philosophy, religion, government, or teachings that present that picture of hope, love and plan for all people?

No matter how good or bad this world is we are visiting presently, just think how great it will be in our eternal home, with a loving, caring Father God, Creator, Savior and His Holy Spirit.

We don't know what he has planned for us in the

long run, but know it will be great and we can all be singing as we go!

Just turn your life over to Him, live for Him and serve others as He did; and the end result will be unbelievable and beyond this world's standards. If there are any real worldly standards? (Reference Matthew 28:19-20) {all versions}. These scriptures tell us to go and tell everyone, making disciples and baptizing them in the Name of The Father, Son and Holy Spirit.

CHAPTER 7

GODS HOLY BIBLE

God's Holy Bible is this world's written Holy Word. It was written by those inspired by God's Holy Spirit. The following is presenting information from early Bibles for you to consider and I know that the only way to understand and absorb God's word is to be looking for

God's directions and Truths.

It must also be read listening for the Holy Spirit's guidance and directions to understand and interpret it correctly. Any other way will lead you astray from His Divine Truths

The following is food for thought and information only. But for those who wonder about biblical Translations over the years:

It is not a manmade set of ideas from years ago. It applies to today, and always will and will never be taken away: but will always exist, according to scripture.

Jesus said "I Am The Way, The Truth and The Life and No one comes to The Father except by Me" (KJV, ASV, NIV, etc.)

God never does anything half way, as He is Holy, Everlasting and Omnipotent, Omnipresent, and Above ALL Creation and Created things both Visible and Invisible (Spiritual)!

Words from First Bible printed in Scotland – 1576

Here is the spring where waters flow,
To quench our heart of sin,
Here is the tree where truth doth grow,
To lead our lives therein:
Here is the judge that stints the strife,
When men's devices fail:
Here is the bread that feeds the life
That death cannot assail.

The tidings of salvation dear,
Comes to ears from hence:
The fortress of our faith is here,
And shield of our defense.

Then be not like the swine that hath
A pearl at his desire,
And takes more pleasure from the trough
And wallowing in the mire.

Read not this book in any case,
But with a single eye:
Read not but first desire God's grace,
To understand thereby.

Pray still in faith with this respect,
To bear good fruit therein,
That knowledge may bring this effect,
To mortify thy sin.

Then happy you shall be in all your life,
What so to you befalls:
Yes, double happy you shall be,
When God by death you calls.

From Dr. John MacArthur's 'The MacArthur Bible Handbook'

AS BIBLE TRANSLATIONS

The following was taken from "Trial by Fire" which is the struggle to create The Bible into English. This study was prepared by Harold Rawlings (Ph.D. Louisiana Baptist College). I have added extra information to some of his presentation. Why, because none of us know it all with the exception of the Trinity. Anytime someone attempts to explain it all, human tendencies get in the way regardless of who it is. So always lean on the Holy Spirit's directions to help us all understand what God wants us to acquire from scripture and don't battle between scripture but look at it all for answers.

It should be noted that every time a new translation came out there were major disagreements and even killings as the writers were considered heretics or evil because of some changes or thoughts that ensued from the new translations. That should never occur with true believers and followers of The Trinity of God.

A short summary of his presentation in the book:

1. The Bible of the Western Christian world started as a Latin Bible, also known as the 1st Old Latin translation. It was very poorly written and a very defective translation, plus very inaccurate. The writers were not Hebrew or Greek scholars thus the errors and inaccuracies.

2. Then the Vulgate **345- 419 AD** was prepared by Eusebius Hieronymus (Known as Jerome). This was later called the Latin Vulgate.

This translation more accurately represented the original Greek and Hebrew text as Jerome was a Hebrew and Greek scholar.

The Vulgate became the accepted standard or official Bible for 1000+ years.

Latin became thought of as the angelic language, divinely inspired and inerrant Word of God.

The first printed Bible was off of the presses of Johannes Gutenberg of Mainz, Germany **1454/1455 AD** and it was Jerome's "Latin Vulgate".

Many even thought of the Latin Vulgate as superior to the original Greek and Hebrew writings.

Latin of course eventually became a dead language when Rome fell as a world power, but the Catholic Clergy, Priesthood hung on to it as that made them superior to the people and in charge of all scripture interpretation. Many miss interpretations were passed on as many of the priests did not study the text and passed on traditions and practices that they did not know where they even came from. The Church, Pope and Priesthood controlled and dominated everything, including many governments in Europe. Some of my thoughts on this subject is that many were trying to protect deviations from the original "Latin Vulgate" and in other cases would be by church leaders of other denominations tending to use scripture to sell their own ideas, without taking the entire text into consideration.

Mankind tends to want it their own way and will push their own concepts regardless of worldly denominations. Only God's way is perfect and we must study and follow His leading, period, as best we can understand it with the aid of the Holy Spirit.

Only the total text should be used and not pieces of it to make some point. Prosperity Ministers are one example of miss leading congregations, because in this world everything is not going to be great, as evil exists in this world. Another miss guided approach is the Five Pillars of Calvinism and modifications by following theologians such as Theodore Beza (1519-1605).

Should be Notes from Dr. Chuck Pourciau' sermon on 8/20/17, plus my thoughts on the subject, which I believe are in agreement about the TULIP doctrine:

The TULIP concept:

A. **Total Depravity**: Being dead in their trespasses and sins, sinners are incapable in their own power of responding to the gospel.

B. **Unconditional Election**: God elects and condemns according to his own inscrutable will.

C. **Limited Atonement**: Christ died only for the elect.

D. **Irresistible Grace**: the Holy Spirit works irresistibly in the hearts of the elect.

E. **Perseverance of the Saints**: God gives sufficient grace to the elect for them to persevere until death.

Where do I believe the Bible stands on these 5 points?

Total Depravity - Yes
Ephesians 2:1 (NASV) "And you were dead in your trespasses and sins,"

Unconditional Election – No
1 Timothy 2:3-4(NASV) " This is good and acceptable in the sight of God our Savior, <u>who desires all men to be saved and to come to the knowledge of the truth.</u>"

Limited Atonement – No
1 John 2:2(NASV) " and <u>He Himself is the propitiation for our sins</u>; and not for ours only, but <u>also for *those of* the whole world</u>."

Irresistible Grace - No
Matthew 23:37 (NASV) Jerusalem, Jerusalem, who kills the prophets and stones those who are sent to her! How often I wanted to gather your children

together, the way a hen gathers her chicks under her wings, and <u>you were unwilling.</u>

Perseverance of the Saints – Yes
John 10:27-30 (NASV) "My sheep hear My voice, and I know them, and they follow Me; and <u>I give eternal life to them, and they will never perish</u>; and no one will snatch them out of My hand. My Father, who has given *them* to Me, is greater than all; and <u>no one is able to snatch *them* out of the Father's hand.</u> I and the Father are one."

What does all this mean?

> **Total Depravity** is in line with scripture as we are all born self-centered and therefore sinful in nature and can't get to God on our own. (Remember ME'ism).
> **Unconditional Election** is wrong because it implies we were selected before our lives began and some weren't. That is wrong because God wants everyone to repent and return to Him and accept His Son, as Savior and Lord. God wants all to accept Him and return His love, but some won't

listen to The Holy Spirits call and leading. We were given free will on purpose, but expect the consequences of incorrect decisions/choices.

Limited Atonement is wrong as everyone who totally commits to God and returns to Him as Savior is not limited, but becomes His children, when they accept and follow Jesus (Ref. John 3;16 and Romans 10:9-10)

Perseverance of the Saints is correct with one exception and that would be the individual rejecting the Holy Spirit. Not sure that is truly possible once we total repented and committed ourselves to our Savior and Lord totally as the Bible says we are sealed forever by the Holy Spirit. The rejection of the Holy Spirits calling us to be saved is like that grain thrown on to the road or in the weeds and never produces fruit. Did that person ever totally commit to the calling or leading by The Holy Spirit? You can't hold back, you're either in or out in your acceptance of His Grace and Gift of Love. No part of you can hold back. Read the book Job as he was tested to see if he stayed true to God. Hardship, pain, illness, loss of loved ones, etc. etc. should not stop a true believer from holding tight to their belief and faith in God our Creator, Savior and Guide. Even our dyeing on the cross or facing deaths door in terrible circumstances. We are to go to work serving Him at His will and direction, not just sitting around listening, but sharing His Love and Word with others. Some call that missions, but I call that a loving desire to be servants as Christ was for the world to allow us sheep to be returned to God (the fold) as a prime example.

In summation on this topic
Salvation is a sovereign work of God from beginning to end.

Man does nothing to deserve it. Neither does he do anything to initiate, continue, or consummate it. It is completely and fully the work of God, and any theology that elevates the role of man diminishes this masterful work of God. Modern Arminians contend that man doesn't inherit the sin of Adam and is born innocent and is so until he actually sins. The original Arminius would be to differ. **Jacob Arminius: "The Free Will of man towards the True God is not only wounded, maimed, infirm, bent, and weakened; but it is also imprisoned, destroyed, and lost: And its powers are not only debilitated and useless unless they be assisted by grace, but it has no powers whatever except such are provided by divine grace."**

God desires the salvation of all humanity.

The passages of Scripture that assert this can be affirmed at face value without detracting from God's sovereignty. However, the desire on God's part for the salvation of all is not fully met. Mankind has been given free will and must accept God's calling from the Holy Spirit.

God permits the damnation of the unbeliever.

He doesn't ordain it. He knows in advance it will occur and permits it. The elect are saved by God's unconditional grace, but the lost are condemned because of their unbelief, their rejection of God's offer of grace. God is not the author of sin. He sovereignly chooses to allow unbelievers to go the way of perdition (Me'ism), but he does not desire it, nor does he cause it. God's choice of the elect is not conditioned upon any foreseen merit on the part of believers. We choose him and love him because he first chose us and first loved us.

Every person has the opportunity to choose or reject salvation.

For this reason everyone is responsible for his own decision and will give an account to God.

That salvation is completely the responsibility and work of God and should be a comfort to the believer. Be reminded of **Romans 8:28-30 (NASV)**

"And we know that God causes all things to work together for good to those who love God, to those who are called according to *His* purpose. For those whom He foreknew, He also predestined *to become* conformed to the image of His Son, so that He would be the firstborn among many brethren; and these whom He predestined, He also called; and these whom He called, He also justified; and these whom He justified, He also glorified."

Back to info from "Trial By Fire" and my comments interjected:

Scripture does not disagree with itself because **God does not argue with Himself, He Knows the Answers.**

3. The Anglo Saxon Bible was the next major writing about **995 AD**. This bible was not English but rather a Germanic language. The British and Irish Island group were primarily Celtic speaking people, which changed over time with invading armies and people (Rome early on, then Germanic people and then Norseman and Normandy invasions (French and Scandinavian peoples). A blending of languages thus took place.
4. The first English attempt at a Bible of any consequence was the Wycliffe's Bible **1382 AD**. This Bible was highly criticized as it was not from the Catholic Church who were in charge of English religion at that time.
5. Erasmus' (Greek) translation 2nd edition, was the next major translation in **1519 AD** and was the primary bases for Luther's New Testament (German) and later the King James Bible.
6. Luther's New Testament (German) was released in **1522 AD**. Luther broke from Erasmus mainly because Erasmus stayed loyal to The Holy Catholic Church, The Pope, and The Priesthood beyond the truth of the scripture, whereas Luther

accepted Scripture as the Gospel over the Pope and any Priest's ideas, practices or customs.

Luther approached kicked off the Reformation and the Protestant revolt, which stipulated and emphasized the simple principle of Biblical Truth as the sole basis for Faith and Practice.

The Catholic Church **at that time** emphasized: sacraments, rituals, complex organizational structures, the priest hierarchy, belief in purgatory, Papal infallibility, clerical celibacy, transubstantiation, popular worship of the Virgin Mary, and finally the worship of The Holy Mother Church itself.

<u>They preached and demanded Works</u>, not salvation thru Christ's Grace and God's Mercy & Justification by Faith alone, but did look for His forgiving grace.

Note: I personally don't believe that we should be unnecessarily critical of other Christian religions, but trying to understand their position and all true Believers are our sisters and brothers though Christ Jesus our Lord. Be loving and sharing with all believers and not fighting about others trying to totally understand The Word and following The Holy Spirit. All so called denominations at times have added some non-Biblical ideas and changed some of those ideas over time: You cannot dance with anyone but your own spouse, can't play cards as it might lead to gambling, you can't work with other Christian denominations, you cannot swim in mixed sexual groups, etc. I can remember when I was 4 years old my grandfather getting on my mother for allowing 4 year old boys and girls from playing in a wading pool together. Sounds pretty silly today, yes?

7. Note: The English Language passed through three major stages in development:

OLD ENGLISH
MIDDLE ENGLISH
MODERN ENGLISH

See attached sampling of Biblical translations over time

There are others out there, but this presents an overview of the variety of Bibles and scripture developed over the years. Many PhDs in Theology have taken on this task and presented their own variations and using various sources.

APPENDIX SIX

English Bible Time-Line
(A Chronology of Representative English
Translations from Wycliffe to the Present)

<u>Date</u>	<u>Translation</u>
995	Anglo-Saxon Bible (Not English, but **Germanic**)
1382	Wycliffe's Bible
1519	**Erasmus (Greek)** Translation
1522	**Luther's New Testament** Translation **(German)**
1526	Tyndale's New Testament
1530	Tyndale's Pentateuch and Jonah
1535	Coverdale's Bible
1537	Matthew's Bible
1539	Traverner's Bible
1539	Great Bible
1551	Bishop Edmund Beck's Bible
1560	**Geneva Bible** (NT 1557)
1568	**Bishops' Bible**
1609/1610	Rheims/Douay Bible (NT 1582
1611	**King James Version**
1616	**King James Version** ("first considerable revision" according to Scrivener)

1629	**King James Version** (revision; 1ˢᵗ edition printed at Cambridge)
1638	**King James Version** ("The authentic corrected Cambridge Bible")
1750	Richard Challoner's first revision of Rheims Bible (NT 1749)
1755	John Wesley's New Testament (a revision of the KJV)
1762	**King James Version** (Cambridge Standard edition corrected by D.F.S. Paris)
1769	**King James Version** (Oxford Standard edition corrected by Dr. Benjamin Blayney)
1772	Richard Challoner's fifth (and last) revision of Rheims NT
1808	The Holy Bible by Charles Thomson (The first English translation of the Septuagint into English and the first English New testament translated and published in America)
1833	Holy Bible by Noah Webster's revision of the KJV
1850	American Bible Society's first Standard corrected edition of KJV

1850	American Bible Union (Baptist) revision of the KJV New Testament (Immersion version)
1863	Robert Young's Literal Translation of the Holy Bible
1876	The Holy Bible... Translation Literally from the original tongues, by Julia E. Smith (the first women to translate the whole Bible)
1885	The English Revised Version (NT 1881)
1901	The **American Standard Version** (revision of The English Revised Version)
1901	The Twentieth Century New Testament
1903	Fenton's Holy Bible in Modern English (NT 1895)
1903	Richard Weymouth's The New Testament in Modern Speech
1917	Jewish Publication Society's The Holy Scriptures According to Masoretic
1923	Edgar Goodspeed's NT, An American Translation
1924	Helen Barrett Montgomery's The Centenary translation of NT
1925	James Moffatt's The Holy Bible: A New Translation (NT 1913, OT 1924)

1926	Concordant Version (based on the principle that every word in the original should have its own English equivalent)
1927	Complete Bible, An American Translation (Goodspeed's NT, J.P. Smith's OT)
1937	Charles B. Williams' The New Testament. A translation in language of people
1941	Confraternity NT (OT published 1948-1959)
1949	Ronald Knox's NT in English (OT 1948/1950)
1952	S.H. Hooke's The Basic Bible (NT 1941)
1952	The **Revised Standard Version** (NT 1946)
1955	Charles Kingsley Williams' NT in Plain English
1958	Hugh J. Schonfields Authentic NT/ Original NT
1959	J.B. Phillips' NT in Modern English
1960	Watchtower's (**Jehovah's Witness**) New World Translation of Scriptures (NT 1950)
1962/1969	Jewish Publ. Society's New Jewish Version (NKV)
1965	The Amplified Bible
1966	The Jerusalem Bible

1968/1969	William Barclay's NT, A New Translation
1970	The New English Bible (NT 1961)
1970	The New American Bible (**first American Catholic Bible** to be translated from original languages)
1971	**The Living Bible** (NT 1963) Note: Bible paraphrased
1971	**New American Standard Bible** (NT 1963)
1976	Today's English Version/**Good News for Modern Man** (NT 1966)
1978	**New International Version** (1973)
1982	**New KJV** (NT 1979)
1986	The New Jerusalem Bible
1989	The Revised English Bible with Apocrypha
1990	**The New Revised Standard** Version
1991	New Century Version/ The everyday Bible
1993	Holy Bible, New Life Version
1994	the Message (OT In work)
1995	Contemporary English Version (NT 1991)
1995	God's Word
1995	An Inclusive Version
1995	**New American Standard Bible** (Updated edition)

1995	The Schocken Bible, The first five books of Moses (Vol.1)
1996	**New Living Translation** (Revision to the Living Bible) Bible paraphrased
1998	Complete Jewish Bible (Messianic Jewish Resources International)
2001	The English Standard Version (Based on RSV)
2001	The NET Bible (first on Internet prior to publishing)
2001	Today's New International Version (NT)
2003	The Message
2004	The Holman Christian Standard Bible (NT 2000)

I know more have been added since 2004!

The Holy Bible can only be understood and absorbed into our being I believe by The Holy Spirits leading us and seeing our Heavenly Father as a Loving, Caring Being that wants our returned love and understanding for now and forever.

In fact many Old and New Testament scriptures answer questions of the other if we are paying any attention. Jesus even updated and made it harder in some cases such as the Ten Commandments. You cannot even think about many things improperly as they are sins also. Can anyone say they have never thought wrong thoughts? We all must repent and follow God's teaching from His word.

I know I learn more each time I study His word and add to my understanding. Normally without losing the original understanding, which personally I have never had happen.

Then we are to Study it, and go out to share it and Our Saviors Love. We are to Love God with All Our Hearts, Mind and Soul and others as ourselves. How can we not share it with everyone else, even our enemies! Mother Teresa was perfect example of that.

Tough to do but that is part of our cross to bear

in emulating our Savior. Our worldly minds get us in to trouble all the time. Are you forgiving of others or see a pretty girl or handsome guy and think in proper thoughts or get envious of someone else's, things?

It should be noted that exact translations from the original text are difficult, as the interpreters or groups of theologians are trying to modify or update the Holy Bible from other languages and earlier times when some words or phrases meant different things than they do today.

I believe all were trying to help people to better understand God's Living Word, and hopefully led by The Spirit to help mankind.

With Humans though some may have been attempting to put their own religion or interpretation into it (Hopefully not though). God in His Power and through His Holy Spirit can still lead us and may even lead us to verify changes that we do not relate to as what God meant. He will always be leading us His meaning and interpretation of His Word.

Note: <u>General information</u>

1. New International Version NIV and new NIV are a translation that is Phrase by Phrase.

2. The American Standard and NAS are word by word translation.
3. Many people prefer the King James Version or NKJV.
4. I personally prefer scripture that when referring to any part of the Trinity, to have those nouns or pronouns to be capitalized. Also if God or Jesus are speaking to have it in Red letters. I generally use the NIV, but usually go back to NKJV for clarification of thought. If I understood Latin I would probably look at Latin Vulgate also.

Please remember I am not going after any particular religion as only God's Word and His way is absolutely true and pure as interpreted by His Spirit to us incomplete believers on our way to Sanctification which won't occur totally until we are called home.

What Does the Bible Say About Itself

"My Word… that goes forth from my mouth…. Shall not return to Me void, but it shall accomplish what I please, and it shall prosper in the things for which I sent it." Isaiah 55:11 (NKJV)

"The Lord's word is flawless; He shields all who take refuge in Him." Psalms 18:30 (NIV)

"The word of the Lord is right and true; He is faithful in all He does." Psalms 33: 4 (KJV)

"The law of the Lord is perfect, converting the soul; the testimony of the Lord is sure, making wise the simple; the statutes of the Lord is pure, enlightening the eyes; the fear of the Lord is clean: enduring forever; the judgements of the Lord are true and righteous altogether; more to be desired are they than gold, yea, than then much fine gold; sweeter also than honey and the honeycomb. Moreover by them your servant is warned, and in keeping them there is great reward." Psalms 19: 7-11 (KJV)

"All scripture is given to you for inspiration of God, and is profitable for doctrine, for reproof, for correction, for instruction in righteousness, that the man of God may become complete, thoroughly equipped for every good work." 2 Timothy 3: 16-17 (NKJV)

"For the word of God is living and active, sharper than any two-edged sword, piercing to the division of soul and of spirit, of joints and marrow, and discerning the thoughts and intentions of the heart." Hebrews 4: 12 (NKJV)

His divine power has given us everything we need for godly life through our knowledge of Him who called us by His own glory and goodness. Through these He has given us everything we need for Godly life through our knowledge of Him who called us by His very own glory and goodness. Through these He has given us His very great and precious promises, so that through them you may participate in the divine nature, having escaped the corruption in the world caused by evil desires 2 Peter 1: 3-4 (NIV)

"The grass withers, the flower fades, but the word of our God stands forever" Isaiah 40: 8 (NKJV)

You and I can be saved precisely because God has chosen us. Not because we are worthy, but because He chose us all.

You have been chosen by God to be His adopted sons and daughters for eternity. When we turn to Him and accept His Grace and Love offering we are blessed eternally forever, regardless of troubles and hardships in this world.

If you haven't, turn to Him immediately as you do not know that you will even have the next minute.

CHAPTER 8
CONCLUSION

We will never know all the answers while here on earth as humans, so consider the following thoughts and scriptures.

Just a few notes to remember as we travel through this earthly existence. Then to do our best to apply God's Word with God's help to accomplish them.

<u>Abbreviated Words from The Beatitudes</u>
(Matthew 5:3 through 14) {All Bible versions}
Some meanings I believe Christ meant by these words/statements, but note you must read text to see rewards.

3. <u>Poor in Spirit</u>
   Humble in spirit, not egotistical and recognizing we are nothing without the Trinity.
4. <u>Mournful</u>
   Sorry and acknowledging our sins and fallacies, plus weaknesses.
5. <u>Meek</u>

Gently controlled strength in Christ and letting God control us as He is our Master and Lord.

6. <u>Hunger and Thirst for Righteousness</u>
Intense desire for God and goodness to know His Will for our lives.

7. <u>Merciful</u>
Having a forgiving nature towards others as God forgave us.

8. <u>Pure in Heart</u>
Pure in mind and thought (tough to control). Our mind, memories and world get in the way.

9. <u>Peacemakers</u> Attribute of God, not peace keeper, but one who helps establish peace.

10. <u>Persecuted for Righteousness</u>
Christian belief bringing about worldly persecution.

11. <u>When people insult you because of God and the Word you believe in and try to follow.</u>
Don't be shy, but serve the Lord with gladness and to help others.

12. <u>Always rejoice and be Glad</u>

We are the only ones who know where we came from, why we are here and where we are going.

13. & 14. <u>You are the Salt of the earth and the Light to the world – but if you lose your Saltiness or hide your Light you are worthless and the world dies.</u>

You are representing God to others as you are His Witnesses and He resides in you as His Temple here on this earth. Tough to keep this world out of the way as it is in our minds and part of our knowledge base.

We need to be all of the above and receive the rewards promised in those words from our Lord and Savior. Note: Read scriptures referenced above for the rewards that are listed. <u>We should not be seeking rewards in my opinion as that sounds like this world</u>. Just accept Him, Love Him and Serve Him the very best you can with God's Spirit helping you.

Why, because of His Grace and Love, followed by our repentance and acceptance of His free offering of grace, mercy, love and forgiveness.

Jesus even told use that he must leave us for now, so

WHY DID GOD CREATE US?

we could receive the power and knowledge that the Holy Spirit will share with us.

Spend a few moments each day pondering what Jesus has done for you. Sing a song to Him or mentally praise Him in your adoration for Him who loves you more than words can ever express. Read Romans 8:31-39.

If you are still not committed or not sure, consider reading the books of John and Romans.

The following Biblical Truths may help you understand and accept Him as Savior and Lord, which opens us up to God the Father and we can receive the Holy Spirit as your partner in this life and forever. He will counsel, teach and lead you forever.

See the following as a guide on various scriptural Biblical issues.

BASIC BIBLICAL TRUTHS

All people want to know the Truth, but some don't diligently seek it.

God does not mind questions, if we are really seeking the Truth. He will reveal it to us according to His plan and our ability to absorb it at the time. Read the following scriptures in your Bible

<u>Seek to know the Truth and the Truth will set you free</u> – <u>John 8:31-32</u>

God's presences is always Known – <u>Rom. 1:20-23</u>

Seeking Wisdom - <u>Proverbs 1:7</u>

Seeking God – <u>Jeremiah 29:13</u>

Hope – <u>Hebrews 11:1-3</u>

Faith & Belief Necessary – <u>Hebrews 11:6</u>

Recognition of Sin and Inadequacy – <u>Romans 3:23</u>

Results of Sin – <u>Romans 6:23</u>

Christ Jesus did it all – <u>Romans 5:6-8</u>

Repentance of Sin Required – <u>Luke 13:3</u> - Jesus Position: Also Mark 1:4, 1:14-15, Luke 3:3-6, !3:1-5, Acts 2:38, 17:30, 2 Peter 3:9

Acceptance of Christ Jesus – <u>Romans 10:9-10 and John 3:16</u>

Sealed by His Spirit – <u>Ephesians 1:13</u>

Never Alone again – <u>Romans 9:37-39</u>

Justified and Peace with God – <u>Romans 5:8 and Rom 4:25</u>

No worries about Judgment, Perfected by Holy Spirit – <u>1 John 4:17-18</u>

Recognizing other Believers, by love they show each other – <u>John 13: 34</u>. Why? <u>Eph. 2:18-19</u> Same Spirit in all of God's Family

We must take care of others; especially our own family – 1 Tim 5:8

Help in overcoming Doubts – Mark 9:24

Saved by His Grace and not by Works - Eph. 2:8-9, but after being saved Eph 2:10 - New Life in Christ therefore good works should happen – Sharing Gospel and Helping others

Power of Hope in Christ Jesus – Hebrews 12:1-2

Our Continual Prayer should be – Psalms 51:10-12 (Paraphrased)
>
> Create in me a clean heart,
>
> Keep me Close,
>
> Continually restore in me the Joy of my Salvation,
>
> Keep Your Spirit with me Always and Guide me

What are we supposed to be doing here and now? First recognizing our sinful nature. Then asking for God's forgiveness and accepting Christ as our Lord and Savior (as stated above) and then doing what Jesus the Messiah said to do in Matt.28: 19, 20 go into all the world making disciples out of others

and baptizing them in the name of the Father, Son and Holy Spirit.(All Versions)

Many ways to be participating in that, but do your part that you are capable of. Each part of the body/person in the family have different gifts, so use those you have to share the Gospel.

CONTRIBUTORS AND THANKS TO ALL

To many to mention them all, but Parents, Friends, Teachers, Pastors, Family, Class members, etc. along with other readings and The Holy Bible.

Many read and encouraged me to proceed and help edit and revise some thoughts:

Notes: Some information added from Dr. Chuck Pourciau sermons with my own thoughts added as his message related to particular subjects and meanings I thought of while listening or rereading.

He also reviewed this book for me and made comments.

RAY WEAVER SR.'S BACKGROUND

Ray was born Raymond E. Weaver to Christian parents in Kansas City, Missouri in 1936. He had a sister and a brother 9 ½ and 6 ½ years older than him respectively. Ray accepted Christ as his Savior at 10 years old and was baptized. He has attempted to study the Holy Bible and follow God ever since with some usual difficulties growing up in his youth and has rededicated his life since, with no doubts about initially accepting the Lord and being led by Him throughout life. Has been a High School Bible Class Department Leader for approximately 10 years and taught both couples classes and men's classes for over 35 years and a Deacon for 20 plus years. He also has played Cornet in a Church Orchestra for a few years and has been in choirs for probably close to 45 years.

Both parents were born before 1900 (1891 & 1899 respectively), and both had tough lives from early ages. His father lost his father when he was killed in 1899 while they were homesteading in the Oklahoma Territory. Ray's mother after 7 years old, lived in other people's houses taking care of their elderly parents and grandparents. Their backgrounds helped me question everything and always seeking answers (WHY, WHY, Etc.).

Ray's father worked his way through to a Doctors Degree in Optometry and watch and clock repair schooling. He also was wounded in the Army during WW1. He developed, owned, and operated a Jewelry Story in K.C., Mo. for 40 + years. Ray also learned to fix watches and clocks as a teenager. Ray's mother worked her way through what was then called Business College. They were married at 30 and 22 years old respectively.

Some of Ray's ancestry in this country goes back before the Revolutionary War. Actually to 1666 and all of his ancestry were from Europe (Irish, German, English, French, etc.).

After High School at 17, Ray started college at William Jewel College in Liberty, Mo with a major in Theology and a minor in Music. He had won the Areon Award in Music in High School as a Trumpet/Cornet player and Librarian of the music library, which was the largest in K.C., Mo. except for the Kansas City Symphony Orchestra. He also lettered in Football.

Ray and his Wife of 62 years were married, in Denver, Colorado and now have 2 children and spouses, 6 grandchildren and 6 great grandchildren and 7th on the way. All of them and respective spouses and children that are old enough are believers in our Lord Jesus Christ.

Ray stopped college and went into the USAF during the end of the Korean War, where he studied and taught Electronics, Computers and Radar Systems at Lowry AF Base in Denver. He and his wife were married in Denver and while in the USAF had two children. He transferred to Ladd AF Base in Fairbanks, Alaska where he worked in laboratory and flight line work on the F89J fighter Interceptors.

After leaving the AF in March of 1959 he went to work for The Boeing Co. in Wichita, Kansas, working on the ASG-15 Fire Control Systems (Radar & Control Systems) on new B52G Bombers. He also returned to college at the University of Wichita with a major in Physics. He later transferred to Seattle, Wash. to work testing the new Bomarc Pilotless Interceptors and returned to college at the University of Washington continuing his work on a Physics degree.

He later transferred to Hill AF Base in Ogden, Utah to develop testing for the Minuteman Missile (ICBMs) and attending the Univ. of Utah studying Physics. This was followed with a transfer to New Orleans area to work on the S-1C First Stage of the Apollo Moon Rocket at NASA's Michoud Assembly and Test Facility in 1964. He now was also attending LSUNO (now known as UNO) working toward a management degree. He was supervising Test Engineering Laboratories performing Development, Qualification, and Reliability Test on S-1C components and systems during this time and managed a Test Engineering Area, electronic assembly and test areas until December 1973.

After 15 years with Boeing, he transferred his work to Martin Marietta Aerospace still at the Michoud NASA Facility developing and testing the External Tanks (ETs) for the Space Shuttle starting in January 1974. He retired from then Lockheed Martin Corp (MMC and Lockheed had a merger) in 2001 at 65 years old having completed 28 years with LMC and his last assignment was being in charge of the Test Engineering part of the Space Station Proposal Team as a Senior

Engineering Manager. Almost all of his working career was involved in Test Engineering, with some time over Tool Design, Manufacturing and Manufacturing Process (Manufacturing Engineering).

Printed in the United States
By Bookmasters